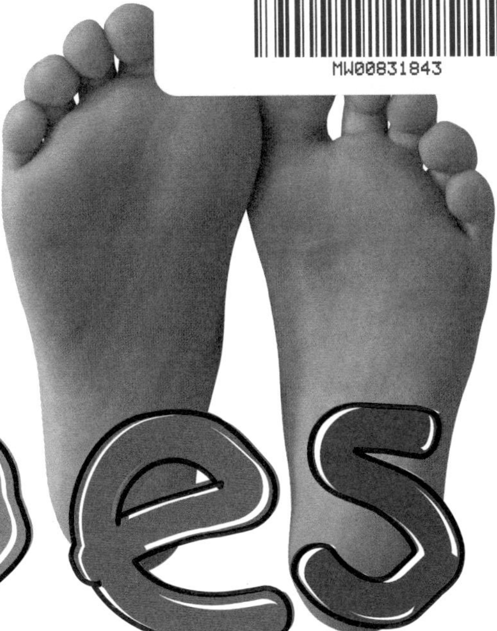

Toes!

Written by Phoebe Wells

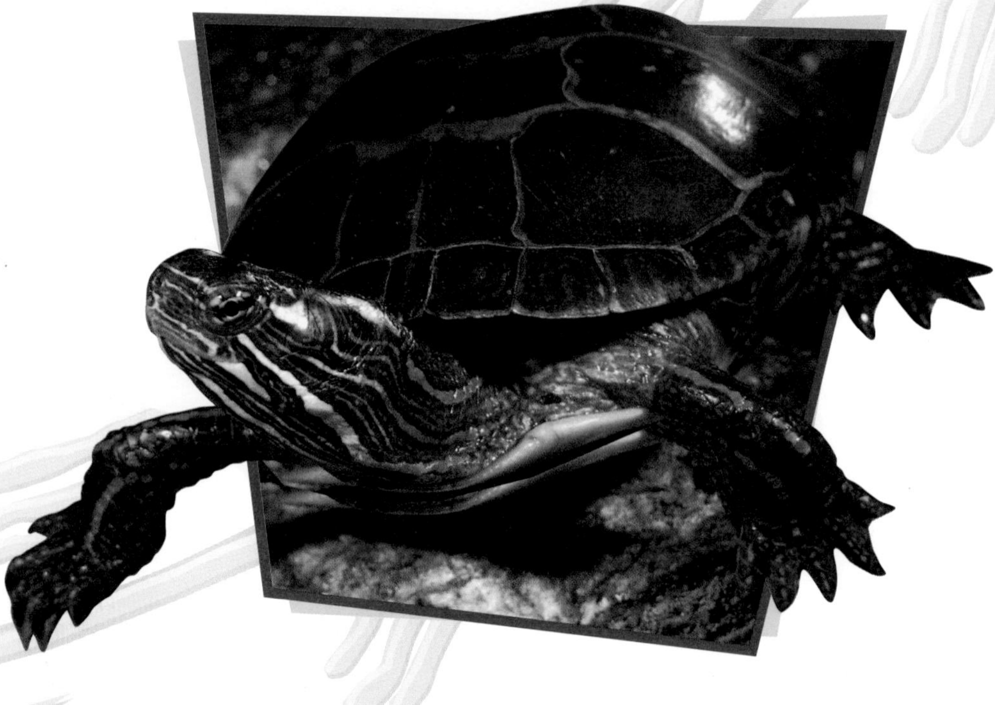

Here are turtle toes.

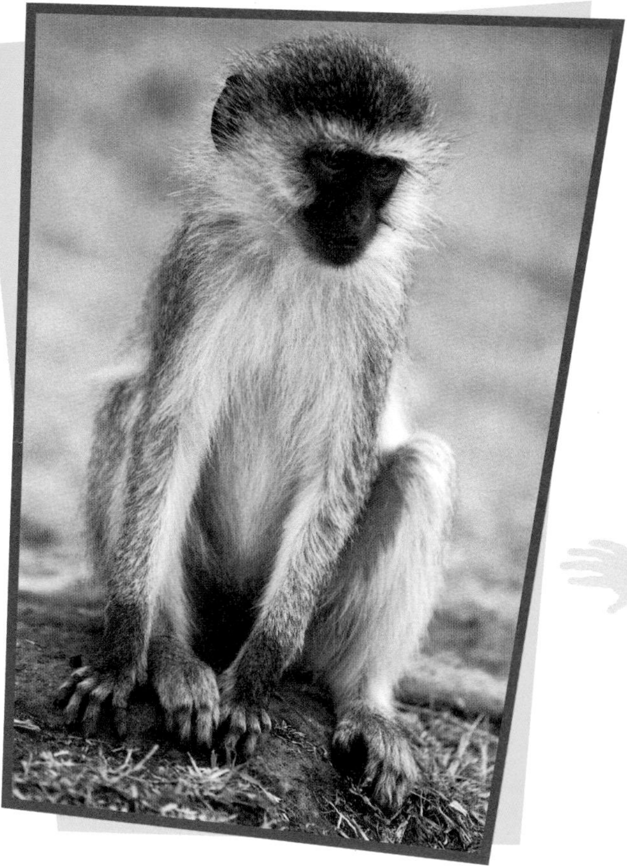

Here are monkey toes.

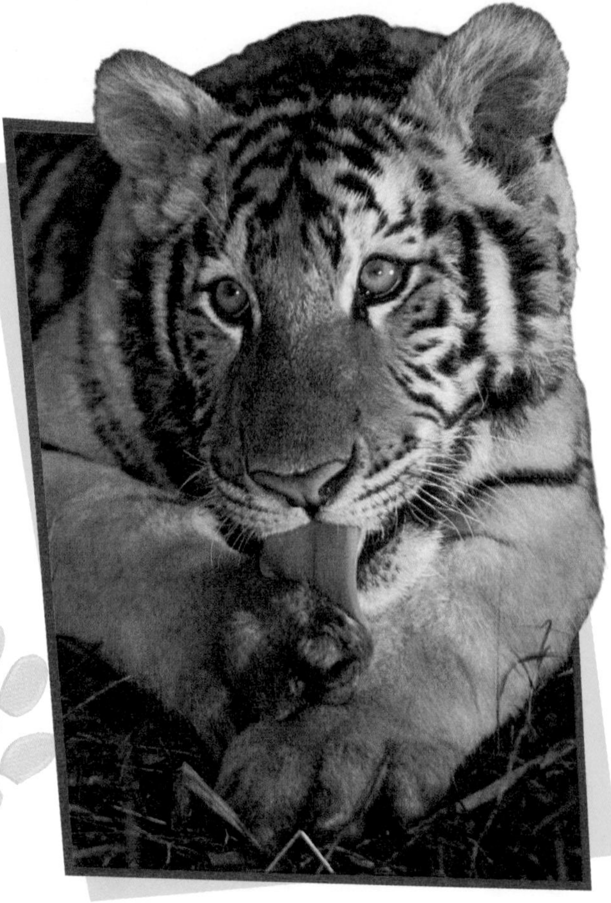

Here are tiger toes.

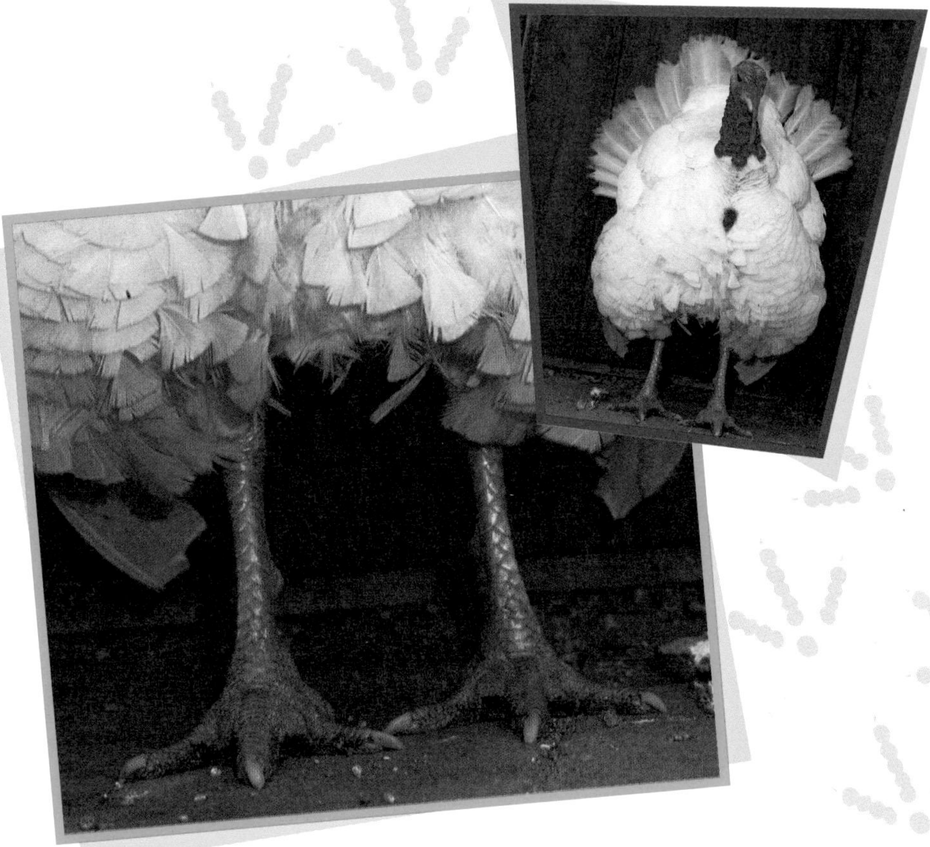

Here are turkey toes.

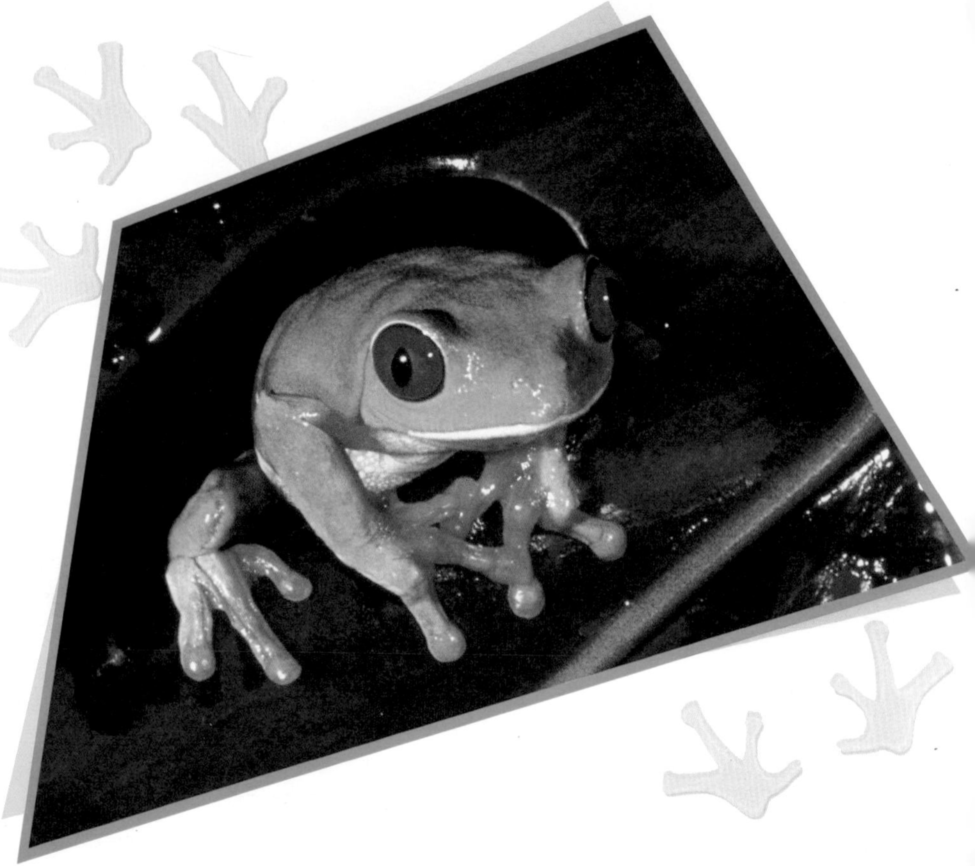

Here are tree frog toes.

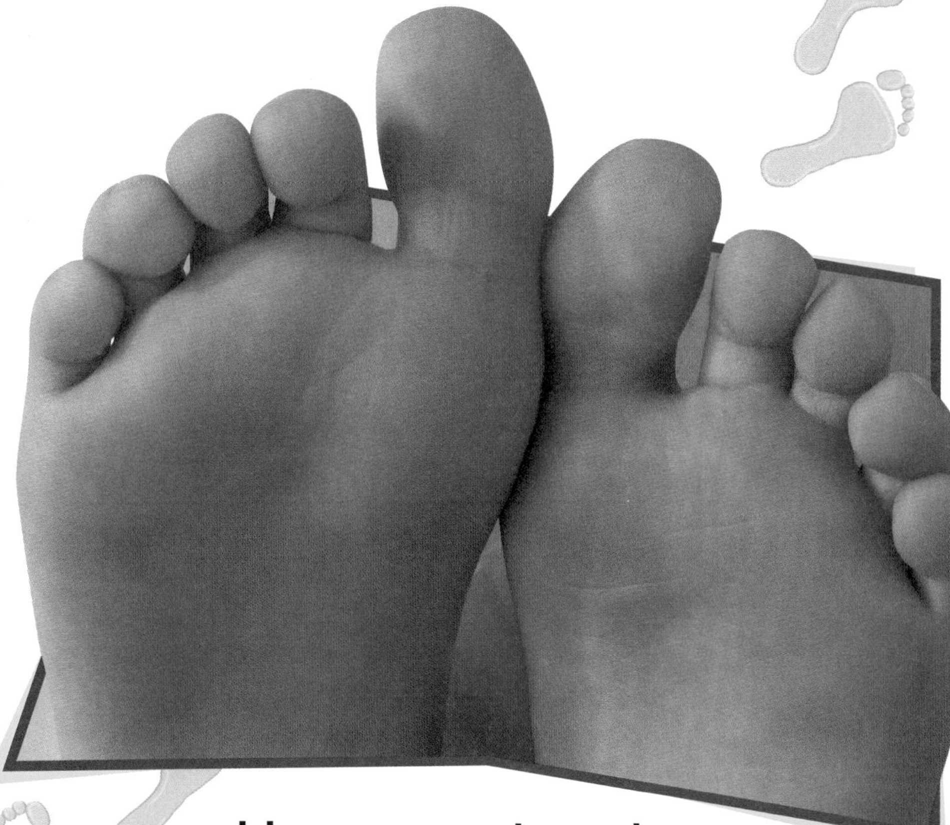

Here are ten toes.

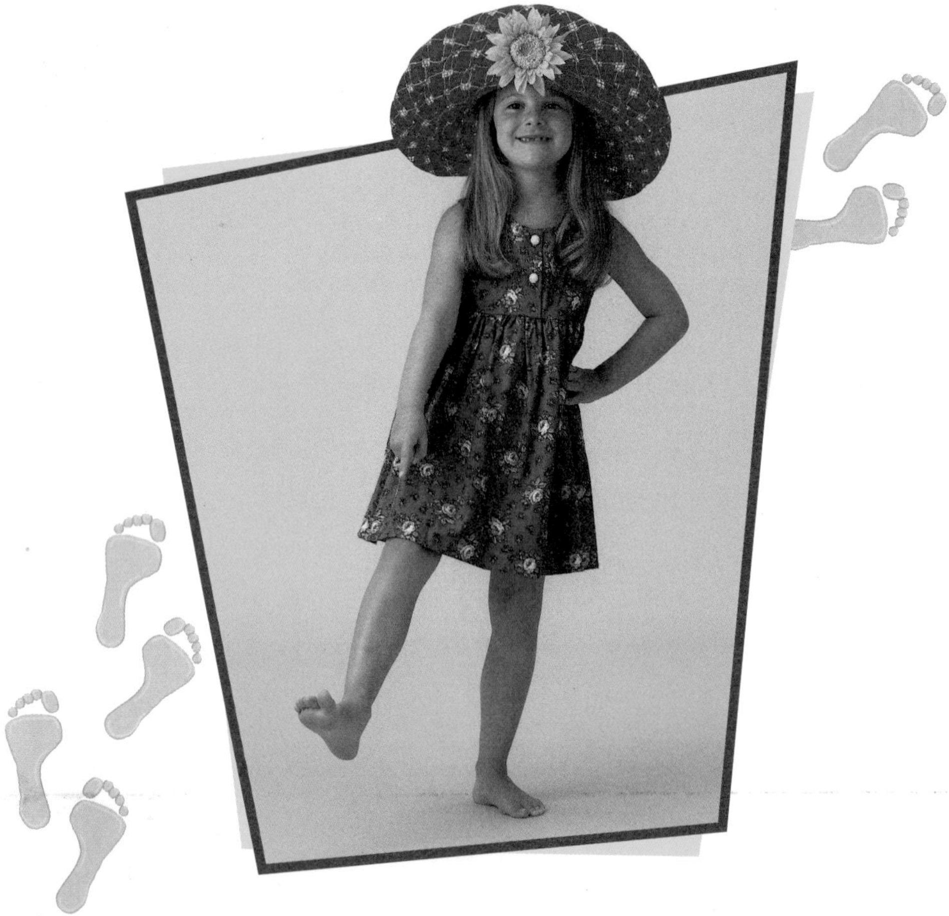

Here are my toes!